SUFFER IN RETICENCE

SUFFER IN RETICENCE

SABERA RASOOLBI

PARTRIDGE

To order additional copies of this book, contact
Toll Free 800 101 2657 (Singapore)
Toll Free 1 800 81 7340 (Malaysia)
orders.singapore@partridgepublishing.com

www.partridgepublishing.com/singapore

Bi-smi llāhi r-raḥmāni r-raḥīm

In the Name of Allah, the All-beneficent, the All-merciful.

As I was born a Muslim, I'd like to use these words to praise my
Creator - Allah, and thank Him before doing anything in life, because
He who has chosen me and granted me His religion, His Mercy and
Knowledge to remember and write this personal work of mine. I will
endeavour to tell the truth, nothing but the truth in my autobiography. If
I err it is solely my mistakes and I ask my God or Allah for forgiveness,
to bless me and guide me from the beginning till the end of this writing.

CHAPTER 1

UNDERSTANDING LIFE

I must explain why I have started with my religious greeting. I was born in a Muslim family. It is said the house that everyone is born a Muslim but the house you are born into makes your religion. My father had taught me a few things at a very young age which made me strong in my faith late in my thirties and have been able to cope with the most difficult times and the peak of my crisis in my life. Since birth until my late 30's I never practised this true religion of *Islam,* meaning *peace.*

Islam came to me after the birth of my third child, K by Dawood. I never understood this religion fully until I underwent the peak of my crisis in the island of Grenada, in the Caribbean. That was in early1990's when I left my house, car and my job in the UK to accompany Dawood, who claimed to have embraced Islam and requested all of us including his first daughter, K aged one year old and my two children from my first marriage to accompany him to read his medical degree in Grenada.

I sacrificed everything to help Dawood because he converted into the Muslim religion by pronouncing the *Shahadah* – a testimony, bearing witness or the declaration of faith of Islam which is the first pillar of Islam, by raising his right forefinger with a witness and a Muslim imam, who leads the prayers in the mosque, by pronouncing *"Ashhadu an la ilaha illa 'llah; ashhadu anna Muhammadan rasulu 'llah"* - I bear witness that there is no god but *Allah*, and *Muhammad* (pbuh) is the last messenger of Allah, made him a Muslim. Dawood made sure that he obtained a certificate from the *Imam* to prove to the Muslim community that he was one of them.

There are four other pillars which are obligatory to make one become a true practising believer. The 2nd pillar is *Salah* (prayer) - an obligatory religious duty for every Muslim. It is a physical, mental and spiritual act of prayer that is observed five times every day at prescribed times. In this ritual, one starts standing, bowing, prostrating, and concludes while sitting on the ground. During each posture, the worshipper recites or reads certain verses, phrases from the Qur'an, 3rd is *Zakah* (charity), alms-giving and religious tax based on income and the value of all of one's possessions, 4th is *Ramadan* (fasting) meaning to abstain from eating and drinking during daylight hours for one month yearly that is when the holy *Qur'an* was first revealed to our beloved Prophet *Mohammed* (pbuh) and the final pillar is Hajj (pilgrimage) - must be carried out at least once in their lifetime by all adult Muslims who are physically and financially capable of undertaking the journey for performing pilgrimage to Mecca in Saudi Arabia.

Dawood did not practise any of the four pillars except pronouncing the first article of Islam, the *Shahadah*. For example, a man who converts into Islam can marry any non-Muslim woman from the monotheist religion i.e. Christianity and Jewish but it is strictly forbidden for a Muslim woman to do so. This is stated clearly in the holy *Qur'an* chapter 2 verse 221. It is strictly forbidden by *Allah* whose command is better for a man to marry a Muslim slave than a rich idol worshipper.

I supposed for a man who is a Muslim will find it easier to guide both his wife and children into his religion. Especially, if the man treats his wife like our beloved Prophet (pbuh) who used to help with the house chores and loved his wives and provided for them equally and made them felt safe, secured and happy.

The Muslim man is the main bread winner and has to build a home for his family. If his wife works, she can do whatever she likes with her own money. She does not have to spend it on the house if her husband is providing and taking care of his family. Therefore any woman would love and respect her husband's Muslim religion and have the children to practise this religion.

Unfortunately, I was trying to get nearer to Allah's peaceful religion while Dawood was running after his friends who were atheists and magicians, instead of working and providing for his family. This is why his 2 daughters are so confused and cannot cope with their daily lives.

They are struggling to make ends meet. His daughter K is seeking help on how to beat depression while he is enjoying life in Indonesia living off investments' interests without any stress. He stole the funds given to his daughters' education by his intimate Jewish magician friend. How can a father enjoy life while destroying his daughters' education and by distancing himself away from them not to support them financially and not to pay the UK government's inheritance tax on a huge fund he never worked for.

Despite all the academic certificates he obtained while living in my house with my support and the sacrifices of my children for him to gain all his achievements, he never worked one day to repay back his father who also invested so much on his unfinished medical degree.

Before his father died in the local hospital in the countryside in the UK, he begged Dawood for a shave so he could look respectable for his visitors, he refused and gave a sarcastic smile instead and carried on reading his magazine about the economy while sitting beside his dying father.

I felt so sad and shocked by his behaviour and treatment towards his father. I went to call for a male nurse who came and shaved his father cheerfully and holding interesting conversation with his father while Dawood carried on reading his scientific or paranormal magazine in order not to feel bored.

His father called me one day and asked me to take his house in the South of France along with a little amount of money which he did not need. He exchanged all the papers but not legally as time did not allow it because he died soon after handing me a letter confirming the house is mine not to his son as he never did anything for him and he left all his funds for his grandchildren including Dawood's 2 daughters.

Dawood was only interested in cashing his dying parent's weekly old age pension and invested their money in his various hidden accounts while living free in my house and by using his father's visa cards for his own pleasure.

Dawood had lived a very comfortable life from birth until his escape to Indonesia with the money investment of his late father in order not to spend on his daughters and to pay the inheritance tax. When he was in the UK he used to scrounge on his parents, me and his obsessed paranormal magician Jewish entertainer.

He drove his disabled father's car round London and parked for free because of the displayed disabled ticket on the car in order not to pay for parking at any places in the city of London. I remembered well we drove his father's camper van to an amusement in the suburb, he would not pay for the car park. We had to suffer before we could enter the theme park as he drove so far to find a free parking space.

Despite all the money he had invested in various banks and building societies, he drove four children and me for nearly two days in his father's camper van to south of France. He would not pay for a place for us to relax at night so he parked in the free car park in the retail centre. It was the most uncomfortable trip the kids had in their entire life. He stretched himself by the wheel and I had to do the same at the back seat with the kids.

As he never worked, he spent more time with his paranormal intimate friend, the Jewish Magician entertainer and his clairvoyant ex-girl. When they were unable to entertain him, he would hassle me and use his daughters to accompany him to entertain himself by visiting all the museums and entertainment parks around London. All his expenses were paid by his disabled father's credit cards. Having converted into Islam, I had to help and support him to do his medical training in the Caribbean island in order to bring him closer to Islam.

Once he had settled at his American medical school with his new friends he reverted to his atheist and paranormal beliefs. He came back from school one day and told me that he did not believe in my faith anymore and he was pretending to become Muslim in order that I help and keep him company and happy in order to obtain his medical degree just like he did in London living in my house. We sacrificed ourselves for him to study and he told me he was not studying for work but to learn how he could preserve his body for a thousand years.

I discovered by his professors that he was contemplating of how to bring his paranormal Jewish magician friend near him, while I was helplessly looking for a place to stay and go shopping with my one year old daughter and hunting for schools for my other 2 teenagers and flat to rent in this new island. Having been born in an island similar to Grenada, I felt comfortable living in it there.

Dawood would travel in the air-conditioned American bus and spend all his evenings with his colleagues in the air conditioned library just like he was used to in the UK. My children and I had to survive in the heated apartment at the bottom of the hill with the local residents. We had lots of mosquitoes, cockroaches and mice around the dilapidated area and at night they would infest the flat. We suffered and struggled to survive without any friends and family support while Dawood was selfishly enjoying his studies with the rich American students and occasionally stayed with them in their hotel.

Dawood was enjoying life fully just like he is enjoying it now in Indonesia. He has never worked in his entire life and he has never suffered from any pressure in life. He believes work is stressful and his parents had worked until their old ages and they had paid enough tax so there was no need for him to work at all.

Today, his 2 daughters 23 and 20 years of age, are struggling to cope with life in the UK without financial support as I had to be separated from them to pay the bills to keep a shelter over their heads while they are studying. They have no one to look after them. They are both going through financial, socio-economic and psychological crisis in the UK while their father, Dawood's advice to them was to think of positive things which will keep them happy in their life.

He never had to worry about money when he was studying because he was staying in my house and all was paid by the local government. From the day he was born he had been looked after by his parents who were professional workers, his father was a headmaster and his mother worked as a chiropodist.

He believed that he did not have to work to contribute to the society because his parents worked until they died with agonising pain from cancer. Life for him had been a stress-free permanent vacation as he is still enjoying on the interest received from the fixed sum invested in Indonesia.

Compared to his life, his poor baby, K, started life very miserably, while Dawood was enjoying his unfinished medical course leisurely in Grenada Island in the Caribbean. She was being bitten by all kinds of insects such as mosquitoes, ants and cockroaches all over her body and we were all frightened by strayed cats and dogs. Sleeping on the floor was even scarier because the place was infested with mice.

I was once bitten on my forehead by a mouse. I supposed this incident happened because I did not have a fridge and having rotten food and left overs thrown everywhere invited those creepy crawlers in the house. My children and I had survived the most miserable life for nearly 9 months in Grenada residing in the slum area while Dawood spent most of his time on the blue bay seaside campus with the Americans.

Grenada is a Christian country living with my 3 little Muslim children in the slum area at the bottom of the hill was the hardest and most unpleasant times of our lives where we had to put up with the noise of the people singing their hymns and the young unemployed taking drugs to drown their sorrows and the poor children whose fathers left them due to poverty. The children would come around begging for left over soap to wash their clothes on the stone.

The technological items were not available similar to Mauritius when I left the island in 1971. That is why I called Grenada my second home in 1993. We are Muslims living alone in a place where there was no '*halal*' - allowed food and all forbidden food such as meat, chicken pork sausage were available for us during the month of *Ramadan* was incredible. We ate fish everyday which was very healthy and local tropical fruits such as mangoes, papayas, coconuts, guavas and other exotic fruits which were available freely so much like in Mauritius Island.

Dawood had no responsibility as he was using his father's credit cards to pay for his own fees, resources and food and he was living like the rich American students. Before moving to Grenada, I had run a charity company in my community teaching the refugees and any unemployed young people who were illiterate how to read and write English Language for free and there were some students who were willing to pay Dawood 20 pounds an hour to teach them Mathematics privately as he held an MA in Mathematics. He refused to teach them saying that the fee was too low for him to teach them. Funny, I have heard that he is editing one page of English Language for 50 pence only in Indonesia despite this large sum he has invested in a long term interest which he earns monthly and this is more than enough to feed himself. I could not live on anything running my charitable non-profit company.

When we all moved to Grenada Island to support him to read obtain his medical degree, behaved the same way on this island. He was looking after himself while my 3 children and I had been living on a meagre allowance from the rent received from my rented house in London. Although living in the slums, we were very happy to be together and among the poor and desperate similar to those of the Mauritian people I was with in the 50's.

I began to enjoy living in that island even more after I joined its French embassy for a part-time job teaching French Language and working as a tourist guide while my children were at school. My baby was always safe with me wherever I went and whatever I was doing. Grenada became my second home as it was undeveloped just like I left Mauritius in the 70's for the UK. Grenada was known to have been invaded by the Americans. I noticed there were no traffic lights on the roads and hardly any police men round.

My worst nightmare and crisis came when I found it unbearable to cope with Dawood who took his daughter just to play and chucked me out of this little house. He told me that he did not really accept my religion because his American friends told him that the holy *Qur'an* was dictated by an alien and the hell fire and paradise did not exist and all these nonsenses were in my head. I had to get help from the local police to get my daughter from him. After he released my daughter, K he left to his air conditioned library with his colleagues.

The next day, I went out the street to catch the bus to pick my daughter and my son up from the secondary school. I met with this new convert lady waiting by the bus stop. She was dressed in black, with black veil and wore long black gloves like an Arab. So I asked her, why she was dressed like that and when I looked at myself, I found I was more undressed with a mini skirt and top. I felt ashamed of myself when I compared myself to her. She then told me she came to this island to pick a free Holy *Qur'an* to learn more about Islam.

Then I realised I was born into this religion and I was ignorant of the religion I was born into and I should go and get one copy for myself. In fact, I got 2 copies of the holy *Qur'an* translated by an author called Yusuf Ali. I started reading it that same evening and I could not put it down.

I read most of chapter 2 which is a summary of the whole Book. As it was *Ramadan* time. The Muslim medical students were meeting in a hall on top of the mechanic shop and were reading and explaining the etiquette of Fasting. They used to buy *halal* (allowed) meat from that same Muslim Trinidadian jewellery shop where you could get a free copy of the holy *Qur'an*.

I must admit that after I read the holy book I reverted to the religion of my father which drove me to obtain a Masters course in Islamic Studies on my return to the UK where I completed a four-year's course, free of charge in a Muslim College, founded by Professor Zaki Badawi (may Allah grant him peace) for teaching me all about this unique religion and I got to understand my religion I was born into. Part of the course was covered by a lord from House of Lords who taught me the Primitive to Christianity religion.

I was taught that in order to become a true believer in Islam, one must love the Creator, *Allah* and His last messenger Prophet *Mohammad* (pbuh) more than oneself and all his/her loved ones only then one will be guided into the true religion. It is only Allah who chooses who, when, where and how to bring someone into His religion, *Alhamdulillah* - prised be to *Allah*, I was chosen by Him and was brought into His right path during the peak of my crisis in this undeveloped island. We and the prophets are here to send the message only. No-one can convert another human being. I only reverted to this true religion in my late thirties and at the most difficult time of my life. I went on the road at the time when I needed it most and I met with someone who was recently converted into Islam and she advised me where to obtain a copy of the Holy Qur'an, whose author is Allah. Only after I searched and read about Allah I got guidance and have never put His Holy book down until I completed it. Every day I read a short verse from the 114 chapters. I had a habit of asking for any wish or anything I need after I complete reading any part of the Qur'an. Allah has always granted my wish if it is good for me and I thank Him for it, but if it is bad for me as He knows best He doesn't grant my wish, I thank Him more for it. His religion of Islam is a way of life. Therefore, I changed my behaviour, my lifestyle of life and submitted to His commands completely. Only then I found peace and happiness until today.

Prior to being guided to this religion, I used to love my mother more than anything else in the world. I discovered I got inner peace and happiness when I began to search for A*llah*'s religion and sacrificed four years studying it and chose to love *Allah* and His last messenger (pbuh) more than myself and my parents and anything else in the world, only then I got guidance and today I cannot be grateful enough to *Allah* for guiding me into His Straight Path. Ever since that day I have been feeling strong and have been able to cope with any crisis in life only with the help of *Allah*.

I also discovered the effects of *Allah*'s holy Book, the holy *Qur'an* had on me and it became my number one book and not Shakespeare's which I always thought was the number one. I was told that Shakespeare is dead but his book is still alive, but I discovered that Allah's book, the holy *Qur'an* is the most powerful and the most alive book. It is a living miracle and a book of healing.

It has an infinite meaning and the more I read it the more I get its understanding. It is said that when you perform your ablution and face the *Qiblah* - the direction that should be faced when a Muslim prays during prayers, where *Mecca* is, you will have two angels sit on each shoulder and read along with you. This is how I feel every time I read this book. This is the only Book that after reading I supplicate to *Allah* for any wishes and He grants me generously.

I feel satisfied and self-sufficient without money and I am at peace without anyone around me. I have an inner peace when I go to sleep and wake up with the same feeling. What more do I need in life but to meet with my Creator in the hereafter.

The holy *Qur'an* is a book of healing and I realized why my father was only able to read this book and understood it although he could not read and write so I found it a miracle he could read it in Arabic and even used to heal people only by reciting some of its verses including the Opening chapter, the 7 verses which are known to be the mother of the verses. Prayer is nullified if this chapter is not recited in every unit of the prayers For example, There are 2 units in the first morning prayer before sunrise, 4 units in the afternoon from 12 onwards until late afternoon another 4 units, 3 units just after sunset and finally 4 units in the late evening until midnight. That makes 17 units of prayer daily. That means one has to read 17 times the 7 verses first from chapter one plus another short chapter from the Holy Qur'an. If the seven verses are not read then the prayer is void. I personally like to read the chapter 112 which means the purity or oneness of Allah. It is the attributes of Allah. My professor told me that it is worth one third of the Qur'an when it is read in the prayer. My professor mentioned to me that he had to memorize the whole Holy Book when he was 7 years old and it was a pre-requisite for him to be admitted to study later in Al-Azhar University in Cairo. He also taught me the history and what the benefits could be gained from memorizing some of the holy *Qur'anic* verses. Besides, one has to read its short verses with some physical movements when performing prayer and have to complete reading the holy *Qur'an* which has 114 chapters once a month yearly during *Ramadan* - the fasting month, in the Muslim Calendar when it was first revealed.

It took more than 23 years for our messenger (pbuh) to memorize the 114 chapters in Arabic and the meaning was also given to him by the angel *Jibreel* or *Gabriel*, peace be upon him to our beloved Prophet Mohammad (pbuh) who was illiterate. I was told to memorize the verses in Arabic when performing my prayers five times daily. There is a strict condition before reading the *Qur'an* in Arabic and to perform prayer. This restriction is to be cleaned prior to touching the holy *Qur'an* and performing prayer, one must perform 'ablution' which is a ritual way of cleanliness just as the angel Gabriel, *(Jibril)* came to demonstrate to our Prophet (pbuh) how to do this procedure of cleaning before reading the Holy Qur'an or performing prayer. This cleaning procedure is called ablution (wudu) meaning cleanliness. Cleanliness is next to godliness.

During ablution, one must wash three times the right hand then 3 times the left hand with water, wash our mouth and nose also 3 times and our face 3 times, then wash the right arm up to the elbow 3 times, then left one 3 times then shake both hands and rub of your head from forehead to the back of the neck with the wet hands and then use your index of both hands to clean both ears and use the thumbs to clean behind your ears.

Finally, the right foot is washed up to the ankle 3 times and repeated the same with the left foot. To complete this cleanliness 'the *shahadah*', the first pillar of Islam is read silently and then face the *Qiblah* towards 'the *Kaaba*' in *Mecca*. Without cleanliness the prayer will be null and void and food and drink are forbidden either when reciting the holy *Qur'an* or while performing the prayers.

I am always puzzled as to why the majority of the most beautiful, rich and famous people I am acquainted with do not believe in *Allah* our Creator. How can a man whom I know for over 25 years and I bore 2 of his children suddenly, forget them and settle in Indonesia just to meditate and practise his paranormal belief after stealing all their inheritance.

Does he ever think about his children who need his fatherly love, educational, financial help and support to survive in such a difficult world? Does he ever think about them when he is eating to the full? Doesn't he know how much he is hurting his family for abandoning them for his self-satisfaction and egoistical pleasure and happiness?

He had no love for the people around him even for those who had helped him when he needed it most. He had never kissed or hugged his own parents. He never called them mum and dad. He called them by their first names. Neither did he ever hug and kiss his own children. All the questions posed above will be illustrated in more detail in this autobiographical book. Does he ever wonder what will happen to him whenever old age and death will reach him?

His children and I have lived to see the fate of both his parents and their agonizing deaths of cancer while he wanted to prolong their painful lives for the sake of collecting their old age pensions. He asked me to do him a favour to cook light and liquidized meal for his mother so she can live longer as he was the one who went to the post office to collect their pensions. At his parents' house he never worked and never paid a bill all was paid by his father's credit cards as he had the same names written on his cards.

My question remains, does he find happiness only by staying free in a place far away on the miseries and sufferance of his daughters?

Yes. We all agree that money is a necessity like commodity but not the only thing in life. Money cannot buy true happiness, respect, understanding, love, children and parent?

I believe that when one has money he or she must share it and be happy and let others be happy too. Otherwise money is valueless. I will explain how I share the life of both my loving parents without money. I was happy without money. I am now more peaceful and happier without money. I believe without love, respect, understanding and caring for others, life is meaningless.

CHAPTER 2

LIFE IN THE COUNTRYSIDE
OF MAURITIUS

Ever since I was born, nine years after World War II to be exact at the age of 3 years old I was aware of the world surrounding me and until now I have seen the changes for six decades. I was born and raised as an infant in the countryside with my big family which seemed to me at the time living in a world of plenty. My father was the sole bread winner of a family of 14 people including my mother's younger sister, her 3 brothers, my stepsister, my stepbrother from my father's first marriage and my 3 own sisters, 2 brothers and myself from my mother's side.

The house was not big and it was made of sheets of metal, mud and straw and we had an open fire with dried firewood piled up ready for cooking food. We had a big pot and pans and lots of dishes no cutlery except some big spoons and big knives for cutting big fish, meat, vegetables, cooking and serving food because we ate by our hands.

I loved being around my family because I always watched the activities round me by my parents and others. Although I was the youngest, I was not spoilt by any means. I witnessed my father bring home the biggest fish and stayed up late at night and helped to clean it together with my mum, aunt and my step sister. My father could not cook or make a cup of tea until he died in his late '60s'.

My father was a special man in my life. In my culture, men did not have to go in the kitchen but they can help only when there are heavy chores such as cleaning big fish, carrying heavy items, doing the shopping and chopping firewood for fuel for the open fire.

He was tall, dark, strong, strict and serious looking. He smiled only when it was necessary and I remembered how he gave me coins to laugh. He loved to see others laugh although he did not laugh. He loved to do exercise by standing on his head for 5 minutes every day. He rode his bicycle, his only means of transport to work. His hobby was to watch the Olympics and gymnastics late into his 60's. He loved listening to anything regarding the religion of Islam.

He was an interesting person whom nobody understood except me during my short visit a few days before he died. I wish I could have met him earlier and asked him how he worked hard and achieved so much while none of his children had managed to do in this world of technology.

I wished to build a mosque on his acres of land which he used to plant sugar canes, other vegetables and fruits. I would have liked to meet all his friends to find out how he used to heal those people who suffered from evil eyes. Unfortunately, all of his friends had passed away. My father was always dressed in safari suit and carried a gun.

His only book was the holy *Qur'an* and he was the most pious man I knew. He had a great voice when he read the holy *Qur'an* I used to get goose pumps and felt very emotional and tears would be filled in my eyes. I had managed to record some of his readings. He was also popular with his friends in the neighbourhood who used to come and recite the holy Book, the holy Qur'an, together.

He would perform some occasional healings with some of the verses he had memorized. I felt safe, secure and protected as long as he was around me. Carrying a gun was necessary for him to protect himself from thieves and wild animals when he was alone guarding his 12 acres of sugarcane plantation.

He married my mother who was very young and innocent. She was not only the most beautiful woman but friendly, kind and generous. Unlike my father, she was not religious because she was not taught by her parents and never went to the Islamic school. She was the best cook and she learnt all about religion by listening to and obeying my father. She was very talented and gifted despite the fact that she never attended school. Neither of my parents could read nor write. Although they were illiterate, they learned many skills on their own.

My mother's older brother told me that my mother was a fantastic, talented and very skilled woman. She could preserve fresh tomatoes for over a year and she died with this secret and skill. Her parents made an arranged marriage for her with my father who also left school at the age of 4 years.

He told me he used to sell eggs in the countryside and his teacher would come home and beg his parents to send him to school because he was very clever and talented but they refused and he worked as a labourer selling what he grew and made himself self-sufficient.

He was wealthy enough to look after my mother and 12 of us altogether. She accepted my father with his two children from a previous marriage. She treated them equally. She was helped later by her sister and my step-sister. Marriage life was not easy for my inexperienced mother. I never saw both my grandparents from my mother side or my grandfather from my father side.

They all died before I was born with the exception of my father's mother. My mother was very busy with her own sister, brothers, my step-sister, step-brother and my 2 older sisters, 2 brothers and myself whom she did not have much time to spend with. Therefore, I clung to my step-sister, who I called my second mother.

My mother was obedient to my father. As far as I could remember we led a happy life with my father in the countryside. I was too young to recall the quality of life my mother was experiencing but I felt there was love and happiness in this precious family. Later, I began to understand my mother who was very wise and skilled because she knew how to manage us all, feed us daily and even paid for my older sibling's school fees. How she did this although she was illiterate and never held a job, was amazing.

Like my father who was a very skilled man, my mother sewed beautiful dresses for the bridesmaids in the neighbourhood and was the best cook in the world for me. She was not as religious as my father but she learned from my father and practised as much as she could. She was not able to teach us girls but my father ran a religious circle in the house weekly and included all my brothers and his friends who would recite the verses from the Qur'an by worshipping and praising Allah together. Occasionally, my father would perform his healing sessions on people who came for help.

I enjoyed living with my big family and the festive seasons were the best for me because I got new dresses and money from my dad and mum cooked the best food, baked cakes and sweets. They played the most important role in my life and I cherished them dearly. It was always exciting and interesting to be with them both in the countryside and city because they were the only loved and treasured ones I had when I was young.

My family was so important to me and I could not live without them. Unfortunately, I had a broken family when I was 12 years old. Whenever my father was free he would make me laugh. I learned the reason for his actions later that my birth brought him luck and he gave me a nickname Sabera' - patience in Arabic. I adored such a big family around me.

My father was always out working hard in his sugar cane field, doing what he was good at, and on his way back he brought raw canes, fruits and whatever fresh vegetables he grew in his fields. My stepsister had grown into a teenager and she hated school. I was 5 years and I used to love school. Despite, being the youngest, I did not feel spoilt at all.

My stepsister learned how to sew, do fancy embroideries, cook nice food together with my mother. She, being my second mum, made me the most beautiful little dresses and plaited my hair so nicely. She used to do piles of ironing and sat on a stool and squatted to wash clothes with buckets full of water. She cleaned the dishes under a running tap and bent over to grind the spices on a stone outside the house.

Today after half a century, I feel privileged to have all the latest technology to do most of those chores for me and for my children. We have electric washing, grinder, dishwasher and cooker, microwave, heating system, air conditioning, electric shower, flat plasma television and small smart phone and internet where we can be in touch with people on earth and even in the moon with a touch of a button. GPS is leading us any corner in the world.

We have electric cars and all kind of assembly machines and robots which can do most of the hard labour for us. I wonder what kind of world we will have in the next 50 years. This I leave for my children to answer in the future *Insha'Allah* - God's Willing.

When I was about 3 years, in the countryside I could vaguely remember about an incident happened while my stepsister was ironing with the hot heavy steel iron heated by burning charcoal inside it. I shook the table; the iron with charcoal fell on my feet.

She got panicked when I screamed with pain; she quickly poured some violet lotion on my little left foot. She looked after my burn until it healed. I still have the trace of my little burnt foot on my size 6 big foot now. Every time I look at this scarred foot, I have a flash back how she reacted so responsibly as a teenager herself. I supposed when you are a child you get healed quicker with tender loving care.

My stepsister did not get any parental love, she had to grow quickly and take charge of the house chores along with my mum. I enjoyed the time of cooking, eating and watching them cleaning up. It was like a feast eating with such a big family every day. My father was hardly with us during the day because he left for work early morning and came back before dawn. Everything was fun for me I got to watch my mum and stepsister cooked a lot of Indian bread early morning on the tower, a flat round steel utensil, which is placed directly in the open firewood to cook this Indian bread. It was the easiest thing to make the open fire at that time. I gathered three or four square stones or bricks and put them flat on the ground and leave spaces around them which were filled with firewood or dried sticks which we found around the house or in the garden and placed the cooking pan on top of the stones and light the fire with a match or fuel such as alcohol or petrol. It was fun!

When we migrated to the city I used to make this kind of man-made fire and pretend to cook meal for my friends in little toy pans and empty tins in the goats' little stable when they were out braising for food. I used their stable to play mummy and cooked for my friends. It was really great fun!

The greatest moment for me was a visit to my father's 12 acres of sugar plantation, I felt like a dwarf in such a large field, holding the hand of my mother. The most exciting at that time was travelling by bus scheduled twice daily. I felt thrilled and elated to be accompanied by mum to visit my dad at work. Bus was the only means of public transport existed for us at the time from the city to the rural area. Taxis were few and expensive.

I loved being with my mum who took me with her as her company to any places be it to the greengrocer, hospital or to my father's workplace. It was always exciting and adventurous to spend a day out with my mother picnicking and eating sardine sandwiches and fizzy drinks like Pepsi or Lemonade at my father's plantation field. I loved to explore the work place of my father's which was like a wonderland filled with corn, okra, chilli and fresh fruits such as Jack fruit, mango and papayas, and the running water via many long pipes from the wells and little long canals which my father built to water his crops.

The wells were a bit dangerous for both_my mum and me. We were forbidden to walk around them in case we fell. Besides we did not know how to swim, we could have easily been drowned if we fell into them. So we kept away from the deep and narrow wells but enjoyed picking up fruits and vegetables to take home.

Honestly, I preferred to live in the country rather than the city with my big family because it was peaceful, fun, always ecstatic and interesting. I never heard my father shout or raise his voice onto my mother except when he listened to my grandmother. I used to visit my grandmother who lived a few yards away from us. She caused trouble between my mum and my father's brothers and sisters.

This was why my father was always arguing with them and we were forbidden to go to their houses and talk to my cousins and my aunts and uncles. My mother was unhappy with my grandmother. My father visited her every day and my mother had to feed her and clean her mud house. My grandma used to favour my father and that caused a lot of problems and conflicts among all the families.

To avoid a big war among them my father decided to leave them and settle in the city. He built a house with bricks, stones and glass on my mother's inherited land in the city and we moved in the new house when I was 5 years old.

Our house in the city was small and simple and the roof was made out of sheets of iron walls with stones and bricks. The colour of the house was white. It had 6 rooms on one floor but the bathroom and toilet were traditional and separated from the house. There was no hot water.

The toilet was non- European and it was used by too many people. I used to have a phobia about our traditional toilet. I hate using it but I had no choice. It was better than the pit latrine we had in the rural area.

The house had a few windows with glass and few wooden doors. The floors were wooden except the veranda was with brick polished red. It had 4 bedrooms with a front veranda was mostly made of wooden frames and glass for lighting. Attached to the large veranda was a little box room. My two uncles had built their own houses next to ours. My aunt, my mother's only sister and all us including my stepbrother, stepsister, my eldest sister, my brother, M, who was my favourite brother, another sister, followed by another brother and myself. We all shared this house. I loved living with my big family when we first moved to the city just like the countryside. It was not that developed but unlike the countryside it was more crowded and the roads were littered with rubbish and strayed dogs, goats and cats.

It was more polluted with scavengers littered the streets but there was more space with a shop and a big garden and large green field in front of our house, where neighbours laid their clothes on the grass to dry. My parents did not mind.

We all could play in front of the house. The most beautiful thing was the mountain. We lived near the mountain. That is why until today I love and am fascinated by the mountains and nature.

The unfortunate thing was when we had a storm or cyclone, the glass in the veranda would smash and the sheets of iron from the roof would blow away and get lost and the roof frequently leaked with the rain water. We would have to look for space to take shelter inside the house. Outside, the streets and canals were flooded with water and fallen trees would be on the road causing havoc for drivers and pedestrians. Sometimes fatal accidents occurred when children and old people got drowned. For me, as long as I was with my family I was safe and secure.

The storm was the most adventurous and exciting occasion for me because we could crowd together in the rooms at the back for safety. The front veranda was a bit dangerous because of the broken glass. As we were going to be indoors for more than two days, my dad got plenty of food which we cooked on the iron barbecue charcoal fire. We did not have a fridge. Therefore, we ate a lot of meat and chicken which my mother got from her own livestock until the storm stopped.

The 4 bedrooms were pretty strong while the front veranda and the small room in the front were not in use. The house was not spacious for a big family of ten, but compensated with a large playground area in the front of the house. There were just a few houses built with more than two storeys which were pretty strong in the neighbourhood.

They were the modern houses with staircases. The poor families would take refuge in the local schools or local government community centres at the time of hurricanes and cyclones. There were not many cars around either. Most people relied on their bicycles and mopeds. The bus was the only form of public transport besides private taxis.

As we had a large unused area in the front of our house, my father wanted to build an educational institution but my mother did not agree with him. His idea did not materialise. My father helped my mother's two brothers to get married and settled happily next to us. Our extended family had reduced to a close knit one in the city.

CHAPTER 3

DRAMAS AND TRAUMAS

The first drama occurred when I was 12 and I was beginning to enjoy life and romance in the city and hated the countryside. The freedom and space and the exploration of nature and climbing the mountain every morning to feed my goats were suddenly being taken away from me and vanished. It seemed that the city had also robbed me of my big, happy and extended family overnight. The scene of watching my father going away with his bike and gun and never to return was too painful for me to even think and write about it now.

It was not the right time for him to go on the day I had my first menstruation cycle. This dramatic and unfortunate situation left me empty and loveless because my mother was to take charge of us on her own without any means of provision and financial support. Some of my elder siblings played a great part in that miserable moment and broke our close-knit family.

All of us should be blamed for our father's final decision to leave us and walk away and abandon us. My 2 older sisters felt bemused by my scary situation. I was innocent and naïve at 12. The memory of my father's abandoning us left me empty and shocked. Before my father's final departure I must add that my mother had 3 younger boys who were born in the city after me. They were more at a loss of our father than me. I was at the age of understanding but they were too young and grew up hating him even after his death. I was the only one who grieved him and now even more so because he left us with a house to live and some of his land he worked on all his life to complete my dream to build a mosque on it for the both of us to earn benefit from Allah in the hereafter. Moreover, I have understood his religion of Islam and able to help myself anywhere and at any time.

My mother was left to feed 8 of us without any form of government help or my father's support. My mum had been left to educate and cloth us without a job or money. She was being bullied even more by all my elder siblings except my step sister who cried a lot in silence because she loved my dad as much as I did. I felt what she was experiencing at his absence.

Soon after my father's departure, both my mother and my step-sister were being bullied by my elder sister F who added to the provocation of my father to leave us. It was a dramatic scene as I couldn't get the attention of my mother because she was extremely devastated and stressed. No one could understand her hurt and agony of being left alone. This was the only man she knew in her life until her short death.

After a few years my favourite brother, M. who was also my best friend took advantage of the absence of my father to stay away late with his delinquent friends and became very mischievous and was also partly to be blamed for our father's anger because he used to steal money and gambled with his unruly friends when my father ran our shop in front of our house for a while.

The first violent and criminal case happened in the house when my favourite brother, M, helped a friend to murder someone in the neighbourhood. My mother was shocked, devastated and very alarmed as she had no means of financial support to defend him. It was horrendous to witness this situation at home and watch my mother's broken heart and suffered helplessly.

Previously, when my father was with us, my eldest step brother fell in love at college and would not study, the parents of the girl came to complain and insult my father. When my father talked to him and I believed thrashed him my mother took his side. He ran away to his biological mother in the countryside and stayed there and never returned.

The second incident happened when my eldest sister began to walk around with her boy-friend after her private tuition and people came and reported her to my father. My father did not hit us girls.

He shouted at my mother and blamed her for our misbehaviour. While my father decided to leave the house and was having an argument with mum, my eldest sister who was spoilt by both my mum and dad, cunningly, went into my father's pocket and brought out some contraceptive stuff just to add fuel to the heated argument between our parents. This action infuriated my father and this put an end to their marriage life.

My mother was left alone surrounded by her unhelpful and troublesome children. She felt it was her duty to bring us up and pay for our education fees and support us financially. She resolved this in renting our small house to some strangers for extra money. I was young and innocent. I never wanted to hurt her feelings and always did as she commanded me to do.

I was abused by some of the weird men by groping me and stealing a French kiss from me. They were as old as my father. They came to take advantage on young girl like myself. Apparently, they had girls as old as me. I never told my beloved mother about these incidents. I wished then my father was with me because he respected us and made us feel secure and safe by teaching us to recite short verses from the holy *Qur'an* for protection. Our neighbours respected him because he used to heal some of them and their children any time of day and night. Once he left us, this security and safety had gone.

My father did what every *Muslim* parent did at my time to send their children to a *Madrasa* - Islamic school where children learn how to recite the holy *Qur'an* without understanding its meaning and because both my parents were illiterate they could not teach us. Those *Madrasas* are still functioning today in Mauritius. Children have to go after school to learn their religion by learning to recite the holy *Qur'an* by rote. I learned how to pray by watching my mother who was ignorant herself.

The only time I knew the proper way to perform prayer was late in life when I did my Masters in Islamic Studies in early 1990s. I learned that I should love my Creator more than myself and everyone else in life. Only then I would get guidance. I only remembered that my father told us to respect our teachers and they came after our parents. Therefore, *Allah* was not the first one in my life until I was in a strange Christian country suffering from my crisis in the 90's with my 3 children without any kind of help and support. That is where I rediscovered *Islam* and from that day my life had changed to a happy and peaceful one.

Back in Mauritius, in the early 60's when my father could not tolerate us anymore. He decided to put an end to his happy and harmonious family and left my mum to cope with us on her own. We pretended to have forgotten my dad just to show our support to our mother. My father was like a hurt animal and returned to his safe place in the rural area and stayed alone with his prayers and reading his holy *Qur'an* and forming his circle of friends in his new neighbourhood.

He was married to his 3rd wife who looked identical to my mother and settled with this woman and her daughter from a previous marriage. Later my father had two more children by this woman who visited clairvoyants and not only had she believed in their work, she practised some black magic on my father to keep her and her children together. She caused my father more harm and grief in his life when he was old, blind, starving and feeling lonely. This wicked woman wanted only the empire my father had built and his money nothing else.

He left a textile factory for them and a nice piece of land in front of his house which he bought in their names. It was too late, when I decided to visit him. He was like living as a stranger among them and as he was unable to cook and look after his health he resolved to remember his religion and found solace in his holy book and his continuous prayers. At night, he slept very little and spent his time worshipping Allah. His family did not care whether he was alive or dead. I tried to bring him to the UK but unfortunately after his pilgrimage 2 years prior to my meeting with him and after an argument with the local government over a piece of land in front of his house. He died with a thrombosis due to anger. He did not have medical care he was left to die. I was fortunate enough to have met him 40 days before his death to record his whole life story. I heard he died quickly with thrombosis and without pain on his bed after his call of nature. Sadly, no-one called for help and he passed away without any of his children around him.

When my father was with us he used to perform the ritual of killing the poultry which my mother raised. Every Sunday was our favourite meal *Briyani*- rice cooked with spice, potato, and meat or chicken. In Islam any animal must be slaughtered in the ritual way or *halal* or allowed way. We must not eat a dead animal. All seafood is allowed except those with sharp claws and teeth and is carnivorous.

The man has to perform this ritual by pronouncing *Bismillah* and Allāhu Akbar - In the name of Allah and Allah is great and slaughter of each halal animal separately, and it should consist of a swift, deep incision with a very sharp knife on the throat, cutting the wind pipe, jugular veins and carotid arteries of both sides but leaving the spinal cord intact and drain the blood of the animal. As both my father and 2 of my elder brothers were not around my next brother, two years older than me had to follow this ritual. I was told it was similar to kosher Jewish procedure by draining the blood of the animal before consuming it.

To supplement the meal, I was forced to go and visit my father on some weekends to bring food which was left over for the rest of us in the capital city. I used to hate the countryside but enjoyed the daily life of my cousin by sleeping in their mud house. I woke up with them by dawn with the sound of the cockerels and the sound of the cows and goats the hen which had just laid their eggs in hiding places and we all went on looking for the eggs. It was adventurous to go and search where their eggs were. Sometimes they were not ours but the hens belonged to our neighbours who came to lay their eggs in our bushes. My cousin cooked the daily routine of the Indian bread or chapattis for my father to take to work.

They would make a big pot of tea with milk and sugar which would last for the whole day and for any visitor who came on this day. I enjoyed the hot Indian bread with butter and hot tea for breakfast. The traditional way of making the tea was the same in the city. Water was kept in a big barrel too. The supplies of water and electricity would be shortened during the days and night time was totally black out. We had candles and petrol lamps at night.

At my father's place back in the countryside I found food was in abundance. Whereas in the capital city despite my mother rented half of the house and raised her own livestock it was not enough to feed 8 children. I felt sad and helpless and wished that my father could come back and stay with us again.

He was a practising Muslim but was furious with my mother for listening to her cousin who lived down the road. My mother was easily influenced by her cousin and some of my elder siblings. On the one hand, she would listen to her cousin to commit the most serious sin *shirk* - associating partner with Allah, which is mentioned in the holy *Qur'an* as great sin. On the other hand, she would follow my father and try to pray and read the holy *Qur'an* without any understanding.

My mother was ignorant about the Muslim religion and she never went to school or Islamic *Madrassa* – Islamic school which we attended when my father was around. My mother learned little with the help of my father. She used to read the holy *Qur'an* in Arabic too. She died in 1975 the only souvenir is still around is her holy *Qur'an* which I tried to read whenever I am in the UK. One of my sisters kept her holy *Qur'an* as a memorable souvenir. My mother was unaware that she was committed this biggest sin by accompanying her cousin to visit some clairvoyants who took her money and misguided her.

I recalled once a man clairvoyant told my mum that I would die in a car accident, I did believe him at the time and now feel revolting thinking that he made my mother worried for a long time by this false prediction.

I am still alive and I had 2 serious accidents one in Mauritius when the car overturned on the motorway and once in the UK when someone took off without checking and hit my car in the middle of the road. I came twice without a scratch but my car was written off. I have been driving all my life and I am still alive.

In our religion to go to a fortune-teller is one of the unforgivable sin which God says in the holy *Qur'an* that He will not forgive the people who commit *shirk* - the deification or worship of anyone or anything other than Allah, the singular God and association of partnership with *Allah*. Those who practise any kind of magic and try to con people by lying to them and steal their money will perish in hell fire eternally. So my father could not stop my mother from going to her cousin and neither could he stop her to visit those fake people.

I was always by the side of my mother and she took me to those greedy, lying clairvoyants. My mother was innocent, naïve and the most loving mum. We kept each other's secret.

I missed her terribly and I did not spend a lot of time with her because she died very young. I have two souvenirs of her with me only a picture we took a couple of days before she passed away in her sleep in the hospital cubicle and her Holy Qur'an which is now with my sister in the UK. My father loved her so much until she visited those fake black magicians who caused more harm to her marriage and broke our home. My father hated her and her cousin for disobeying him. She was not able to understand my father's healing power.

The Healing Power of my father consisted of the following. After performing his ablution he would recite the protection of *Allah* from the *Satan* - devil the power evil force by saying, *'A'ouzoubilahi minashaytan ir rajeem* - I seek refuge in *Allah* from Satan the outcast, must be said by every Muslim before reading the holy *Qur'an*. Followed by *Bi-smi llāhi r-raḥmāni r-raḥīm* - In the name of *Allah*, the All-beneficent, and the All-merciful. My father used to read seven times *Surat Al Fatihah* the first chapter or the opening chapter of the holy *Qur'an* which is known as the mother of the holy Book with 7 verses. Without ablution any reading from the Quran either to heal or pray by a Muslim person will be nulled and void. My father used to read this chapter seven times and blow 3 times on the person who was possessed by evil spirit. After reading seven times the 7 verses of the opening chapter 1 of the holy *Qur'an*, followed by reciting three times the other chapters or *Surats*112, 113 and 114 plus the

The most powerful words from my holy Qur'an chapter 2 verse 255: *in the name of Allah, the most Gracious, the Most Merciful 'There is no deity except Him, the Ever-Living, the Sustainer of [all] existence. Neither drowsiness overtakes Him nor sleep. To Him belongs whatever is in the heavens and whatever is on the earth. Who is it that can intercede with Him except by His permission? He knows what is '[presently] before them and what will be after them, and they encompass of a thing of His knowledge except for what He wills. His Kursī* (Throne) *extends over the heavens and the earth, and their preservation tires Him not. And He is the Most High, the Most Great.'* which he would read 7 times then he touched the patient's head who is possessed and demanded the evil to leave his/her victim or accept Islam.

The evils cried because they didn't want to be burnt with continuous reading of the holy *Qur'an*. So sometimes some of those *Jinns* or evils leave and never come back to possess their victims again while others become Muslim and don't harm people. Other patients with various ailments came to my father any time to seek for help.

That is why after so much sufferings and abuses from my past relationships who never practised Islam I held on to the action which my father used to do and that had made me become strong, self-sufficient and able to cope as a single mother with my 4 kids on my own. Everything I achieved in life was only by the help of *Allah*. May *Allah* grant both my parents paradise for bringing me into this unique, peaceful religion?

The gift that my father left for me is the most valuable one which is helping me to cope with my life every day and able to face with any hardship in life. That is why a sincere Muslim must love his/her Creator, *Allah* and His last messenger, Prophet Mohammed (pbuh) more than himself/herself, parents, and loved ones, only then she/he will become a true Muslim and get guidance from *Allah*. Allah provides and grants anything you ask for without anything in return but to praise Him and worship Him alone.

I am still searching for my partner who loves My Creator, His last Messenger (pbuh) more than himself and all his loved ones. I was told by my professor that if I don't have my partner on earth I will have one created for me by Allah in the hereafter and life with Allah will be eternal. I am very patient like my nickname so I will wait until that time comes.

In the United Kingdom (UK), I had lost my most loving mother in the late 1970's and my younger brother who was born with a hole in his heart, survived for 50 years with an artificial aortic valve replacement until he died in the UK in the 1990's. Whereas both my beloved father died peacefully and my favourite brother was murdered in Mauritius in the late 1960's.

My life in the UK was the most troublesome, when I came to work there. I experienced the direst time of my life. I came with a group of my friends from Mauritius; we were picked up by our manager from the airport and driven to the old people home in the town called Lewis, Sussex. All I saw on the first day were farms and animals and all the houses looked alike. It was like going to a prison. The food was all salad every day and egg or chicken occasionally. I felt I was eating grass. We were used to eat savoury rice and meat, chicken, potatoes and salad with every meal. Not just salad on its own because the cafeteria had only salad left when we went to lunch or dinner.

We had been given a bike to ride to the local post office where we bought egg for one penny. Everything was cheap. I got 60 pounds a month. I sent 16 pounds to the bank in Mauritius to pay for my airplane ticket loan. I sent 20 pounds sterling to my mother and the rest for my food and occasional shopping in the big town called Brighton. It was the hardest work and most difficult time I experienced in the hospital with patients who were senile and obese.

We had a matron who ordered us to work most of the day with only one day off per week. Sometimes we were so tired that we did not do anything just sleep to get ready to work the next day. We had a little room and we were not allowed to bring male visitor in our home.

At the old people hospital, we worked so hard and looked after the (geriatric) patients or old people, who were helpless like babies. Their backs were full of sores because they were bed- ridden or wheel- chair bound. Our duty was scheduled to shift work meaning one week night and the other week day duty. We had to wash and feed them. At night we had to turn them every two hours on their sides to prevent them from getting sores on their bodies.

The geriatric patients were overweight, very rude and racist. They would swear at us and tell us to go back to our country. We were so thin and weak. We had to feed them like babies and then toilet them and lift them to their beds or chair. Very rarely we had to hoist them to and out of bed or bath only if they were very heavy and they were impossible to lift with two of us. The hoist machine helped us not to damage our back. When they were asleep the matron came round and ordered us to clean their commodes (their mobile toilets).

For dressing their sores in their backs really needed stitches rather than stuffing them with cotton wools and apply sterilized dressings to heal. I supposed there were not many doctors available to this kind of treatment. Unless when they reached over 70s they were terminal cases and put in old people homes to die. While working with them I hardly saw their children come to visit them but they were the first ones to come to claim their valuables at their deaths. Those old people who served in the wars were hardly visited by their loved ones and children who lived far away from them. They had many interesting stories to tell. Their sores were horrendous sights when we treated them they yelled with pain and verbally abused us by telling us you black nurses go back to your country. I could not tell my loving mum back home because I was working with these patients to help her and my 3 younger brothers to pay for their education.

When we got home from duty, my friends and I used to hug each other and cry. We were so lonely, unfed and felt exhausted with work. In the evening, when we had little time together, there was nothing to do as we were surrounded by farms. All we could see were animals and the old people. At night, on our night shifts, we had a few deaths in the wards and we had to wash their bodies and carry them or push them on a trolley to the mortuary. It was so cold and scary inside the mortuary. It was like living in hell for a year.

Then we got to do our nurse training in the School of Nursing near the seaside where we did not have much time to spend as we were working and training so hard. After two or three years, I met my husband in one of the psychiatric hospitals nearby. After a few months we went to Mauritius to get married. After marriage, I did not feel like he was treating me like his wife for he showed how much he cared for his mother and his sister alike. He would send most of his salary to Mauritius. He never tried to rent a flat outside his campus to live like a married couple. He was more worried about how to please his mum and sister back home in Mauritius. Whatever money was left it was for entertaining his psychiatric colleagues with drinks and parties. I supposed that is why he has been running his off-licence and grocery store in London until now as he is good at it. In Islam, it is forbidden to drink or sell alcohol. I was so pleased I didn't have to involve myself in this kind of work for money. I felt nursing was a rewarding job at the time.

My wedding was a double one because my brother who was two years my senior, a policeman decided to get married at the same time to save money. I did not feel I was married when I returned to the UK. I never felt settled because I was living as a single woman and working in the previous campus with him, not as a conjugal married life. It was like living in a secret and uncomfortable place. My nursing campus was stricter than his. So I had to be very discreet when I visited his campus which was full of men.

The marriage was on the rock from the beginning. It may be because of our living condition. I suffered too many insults and racist remarks from my in laws although they were miles away from me. In fact, they were 6,000 miles away. My ex-husband received letters from them advising him to leave me because I didn't match their family, I am black and ugly 'madras', people from southern India who have dark skin. They would insult my mother back home in Mauritius by harassing her to tell me to leave their son and brother because he was too white for me.

I suffered from stress and was never at peace with my mother-in-law, father-in-law who was a taxi driver and every time he passed my mother he would stop at mother's house by swearing at her ordering her to tell me to leave his son and my ex-sisters-in-law would write to me and tell me the same message and added that I was not fit for their brother. These were the causes of the breaking of my marriage. I never regretted having divorced my ex-husband. I was liberated and enjoyed my freedom and life was more interesting, exciting and enjoyable being a single mother with my son and daughter, working, studying and bringing up my two young babies kept me busy and occupied.

The previous bad experience did not stop me from falling into another two worse relationships that made my life even more difficult and unbearable. One of them was a handsome artist/architect student who came to use and abuse my generosity and the other one who was obsessed in everything there is in life. He was studying for pleasure and practising what he liked best in his life in comfort out of the miseries of others. More about them will be illustrated in the next chapter.

CHAPTER 4

EXPERIENCES OF MY EXOTIC AND CONFUSED LIFE

From a very young age I began to suffer from an inferiority complex because of my dark skin. I was always ignored when my mother's cousin and her family came to visit her. I was hiding because of the colour of my skin. Most of my mother's nieces were very fair and well-off. They lived in big houses and owned their own cars. Some of her relatives had holiday houses on the beach with boats. I was not welcomed at their places. I quickly learnt at a very young age that those fair skinned girls got more attention and without any education they were married off to rich men and some others with professional skills abroad such as doctors and teachers, came to marry those fair skinned girls and take them abroad for a better life.

In the city we all had to go to school. At the age of five, I started nursery which I hated because it was a co-education nursery school and my elder siblings used to tease me if any little boys came to call me while the teacher waited outside with the rest of the pupils. For that reason, one morning, I refused to go to school with the little boy who came to pick me up. My uncle gave me a good beating with an electric wire and then gave me some sweets and fruits to make me feel better. I went with the boys to school. I had no friends to play with after school because my father was very strict and the parents of the Chinese tenants in our shop were strict too. I could only ride a borrowed bike with my own brothers and sister.

Well, my two uncles got married and seemed to be happy. They lived next to our house. They minded their own business. My mother was pregnant again three more times after we moved to the city. I had another 3 brothers which meant I had lost all the attention of my parent. My father loved and adored my two younger brothers. He loved my mother for the two sons she gave to him. Every evening I noticed my father sat under the big banyan tree with my 2 little brothers on his lap and my mother at his side talking until dark time. I felt I was being ignored but glad to see my mum happy with my father. I felt a bit rejected but my step-sister was the only one who gave me enough attention. She helped me with my homework spelling test and dressed me nicely to go to my primary school.

Life in the city began to cause friction at home. My father was under pressure to keep his French boss happy with money which he did not have. He had to take loan after loan to keep the French sponsor happy. All the pressure he was facing affected all our education and our living standard. He had no one to support and help him. His eldest son had run away from our house and the other one, my favourite brother, was causing him more stress by stealing money from his shop and gambled with his friends. Although he lost little sum playing cards with his friends, he always got a good beating by my father.

When I was 12 years I had to watch my father packed his things and left the house for good due to the demand and stress put upon him by my elder siblings and my mother was against him for taking sides of my elder ones when my father disciplined them. My mother was always kind and lenient towards us all. I can never forget that day, I felt my world ended. My mother was in tears be over a big argument due to my siblings not obeying my father and helping him. He had to pay for their colleges and tuition fees and at work too much expectations and demands from his French sponsor who provided him with machinery and helped him with his harvest of sugar cane to the sugar mill factory.

To add to his anger, my mother went against him by consulting some clairvoyants. My father believed my mother had been influenced by one of her distant cousin who lived down the road. So my father warned my mother not to go to her as she was committed the greatest sin in Islam. My father was very pious. When my father got so furious my aunt called him 'a big, bad, black wolf'. My father could not tolerate my mum following her cousin to fake clairvoyants and take our sides when our father tried to discipline us. That made him furious and unable to cope so he walked out the house.

Life became a misery for us all. My mother had no means to pay for our colleges and exams fees. She had to rent half of the house in order to feed us. She raised her own livestock and fed us with eggs and poultry. I used to take the goats up the mountain and enjoyed the morning walk and had fun with the rest of my siblings. When my father was with us I was not allowed to play with my neighbours children. When he left I got to play with new friends at college and I walked the citadel, a little fortress, where the guards kept an eye on the city.

I too discovered freedom to do as I pleased and took advantage of my father's absence and enjoyed longer hours playing with my friends at college. I used to fancy someone whom I would meet in the library on Saturdays. It was exciting to go to the library to study and have fun after in the secluded places such as hills and play grounds. I supposed I was copying what my elder sister used to do. I used to get hurt for the person sometime I really liked was not interested in me. I supposed I was too young but missing the love of my father. My father had left. I was in search of a fatherly love. He had snatched my happy world of teenager and disappeared.

I felt a great loss in my life due to my father not being around and at the same time I was enjoying my freedom without him. I used to dwell on the memory of my father who was very religious and a healer. I missed listening to him reciting his only holy Book, the holy '*Qur'an*'. The people who came round sought his spiritual help. Thursday evening was the best day apart from Friday he would have a circle of friends who came round and stayed till late supplicating Allah in our veranda. Sometime my brothers would join the circle. Men from the neighbourhood would walk in any time for spiritual healing. My father usually read some holy *Qur'anic* verses on me at night when I had nightmares.

Although he was strict and disciplined I loved him and part of my life was missing until today and I love him more today than when he was alive. He was very talented and skilled in his field of work and also his recitation of the holy 'Qur'an' in Arabic, was a miracle although he was illiterate he used his skill to heal people. Listening to his recitation of the Qur'an used to give me goose bumps. I was not able to show him my love and appreciation. After he left us I was unable to speak to him when I saw him in the street. It broke my heart seeing him sitting at his friend's tailor shop waiting to see us coming back from college. We zoomed by him pretending we did not see him, he went back feeling hurt. He was respected by his friends and our neighbours because he was a healer. Suddenly, he became a stranger in the neighbourhood and especially to me.

A few years after my father's departure, my eldest sister got a job as a training nurse and my brother one year older than me got a job in the police force. They started bullying my mother because she depended on them for bringing a little money home. The meagre salary they contributed wasn't enough for my mum to prepare their lunches for them to take to their work.

Thank God my mum was skilful enough to bring more money at home with her embroidery skill, she would do the 'trousseaux,' the bridesmaid clothes in the neighbourhood. She used to sell part of her livestock and with the rent of half of the house and also she used to grow organic vegetables in our big front garden which she sold to the neighbours. She struggled until both my sister and I left to go to the UK to work.

Prior to my departure to the UK, I was being abused by the male lodgers in our house. I never told my mother about those abuses. The only one she knew was one of the handsome young man who used to follow me when I was at college. His intention was to marry me and keep me in the community. My mother and I had other plan for him. He was one of the heroes in the neighbourhood protecting the local minister as a bodyguard.

I was 17 years old attractive, slim, dark and very friendly. This handsome man who wanted to marry me was really harassing me by coming to my neighbourhood and parked in the street to watch me. I was not comfortable with his behaviour but I liked his good looks, his fashion and trendy clothes and sports car. At weekends, he would often park in from of my house and demanded my mother for my hand in marriage.

My mother was very diplomatic with him because he threatened he would take me by force, in other words, he would kidnap me if my mother refused. His family came and begged my mother to marry me with him as their son had promised to turn over a new leaf and start to a new life as a respectful practising Muslim. Therefore my mum, being my best friend, advised me to pretend to love him. When he was travelling with the politician I could run away abroad. That was exactly what I did in the early 1970s.

My mother used to come to the cinema and sat behind me while my handsome hero and I watched the Indian film which I did not understand. He was happy and had great hope that I would be his future wife. He took me and fed me every weekend and gave me lunch prepared by his mother and sisters who were amateur chefs. His family loved me so much because their son had been tamed and stopped acting as a political gangster in the community.

He did not fight on the street for any political reasons and he stayed at home and planned to build a home for us. During *Ramadan* – Islamic calendar month, the fasting month, he would come after the late prayer, to spend time with me. He was the most handsome guy I had ever met. I broke his heart because I did run away when he was not around.

I went to the UK. He joined the Navy and did not get married. After I got married with the first guy I met in a psychiatric hospital in the south of England. I met with my hero I ran away from, visiting his brother in one of the hospital campus where I was visiting a family friend with my husband, my sister, brother in law. There he was standing watching me. I had mixed feelings thinking he came to revenge and kidnap me as he warned me before. I was scared but still had some infatuation feelings for him.

Now while writing I have a feeling of regret because I knew he was a great good-looking, handsome man who was brave to defend both his community and family. They were the only people who never showed me any racism despite that they were all fair skin people. I was treated like a princess. I left him and escaped to the egoistic, selfish and heartless men in the UK. I was three times hurt and left with two generation of children to bring up on my own. I learnt he met someone else on his return to Mauritius and he settled down with someone else. Every time, I visited Mauritius I yearned to see him to ask him for forgiveness. I hope one day I will get this opportunity. This love story ended very emotionally for me.

In the UK I was not happy with my own siblings again they were all there. In fact, one of my brothers, Joe, helped to break my marriage and he honoured them by marrying my ex sister in law who used to abuse me verbally and he is still with them. They are enjoying life to the full as they had money by selling alcoholic drinks in their grocery shop.

They were able to send their children to private schools and they lived a good life. While I was struggled to make ends meet with my two kids. As a single mother, life was really hard and challenging for me as I was studying for higher education, looking after my kids and working to pay the bills. I did not have any support from any of my 3 brothers who were married and lived their own lives with their wives. My sister who resides in the UK also supported my brother and his new family who consisted of my ex-husband and his new wife.

I felt life was like a poison and I had to drink it. My children were growing without any relatives and their father's support. I did well in my first degree studying government policy in Planning and then obtained my Masters on Media and Communication policy studies specialising in Radio and Television. I studied for another Masters in Islamic Studies in 1992. Followed by Teacher Training PGCE and CELTA. My aim was to travel abroad to work which I did. That is when I left for Saudi Arabia.

The agony I suffered increased when bad luck struck me again. While working late in the centre of the city I met a Sudanese journalist who met me in the stationary shop and fancied me. I did not want to get married again after my divorce. I was a good friend to this journalist who resided opposite my work place. Apparently, he worked for a Saudi prince.

He was so kind and generous to me. He used to buy my shopping and delivered to my house. He used to invite me at the weekend to visit the prince's 150 horses in New Market and we had a fantastic time there. We were served and looked after by many Sudanese male servants and there was a big swimming pool where the prince and his guests including some American women and British girls who entertained themselves. I have learnt in Saudi this has become a normal life for the rich Saudi in the Compound.

This Sudanese journalist was very religious and he prayed everywhere in the parks and anywhere at prayer times. I learnt about his life in various meetings, he told me he had 4 wives in Saudi Arabia and he was editor of one of the Arabic newspaper and furthermore, he kept the prince company who lavished him with cash. Well, I experienced his acts of dishonesty many times. When he invited me to spend a weekend with the prince and his workers to visit the horses and then he would join his male partners at night and stayed with them.

Several times he would invite my children to have a meal in various hotels, where he would disappear in one of the rooms. I caught him once half naked in one of the guest who rented the whole floor of the hotel. I went upstairs looking for him to say goodbye. I ran the hell out of that place and drove off with my kids back home. It was disgusting to see such a religious man with 4 wives and children in Saudi to behave in an auspicious and indecent way. I was even more shocked when I saw him drinking strong alcoholic drinks. I never knew that a Muslim man could behave in such an un-Islamic way.

I decided to take a trip to Spain to forget about these bad memories in the UK. On the train to Madrid I accidently sat on the wrong seat but it turned out to be an exciting and memorable journey because the articulated handsome Moroccan artist/architect did not mind me taking his seat but on the contrary he requested that I stay and asked his male partner to exchange his seat to mine so that I could keep him company all night.

His intellectual conversation was so sophisticated and interesting that I forgot all my worries and unhappy experiences until I reached my destination in Spain. I enjoyed such a peaceful and happy relaxing week in a beautiful place which was full of tourists like in Mauritius. After I returned to the UK, my handsome Moroccan wrote to me about his holiday in his country. Then two weeks after his return to Belgium he came to visit me in the same weekend.

This handsome young man was another person who was very smart and cunning came to my life for his own selfish benefits. He was in a great financial difficulty to carry on with his study in Belgium. He used his intellect and artistic talent to win my heart to support him. He loved his Berber sect or culture and from the beginning he made it clear that they marry their own girls and live together in their own tribal system. I had no culture but strong belief in my faith. What my parents taught me and the way they behaved was my way of living.

My mother and father without any education always helped people with their problems for the love of our Creator. I tried to do the same when I met those men but they turned my life into turmoil. Well, for the second gentle French speaking artist/architect student, I tried to help him out of the sacrifice of my young son and daughter. He too was scrounging selfishly when he came for the weekend he took all my children's food, materials and clothes from them. He came to buy the latest fashion clothes, camera and books for himself and his room-mate whom I met in the train. All his shopping was paid by my hard-working money, leaving my darling children deprived of the basic things. In my religion it says you give with your right hand while your left hand is unaware of your action. Later I discovered that he was using my generosity and hospitality for his own materialistic purposes. When I think about it after many years I discovered that I was made a victim because I was young, naïve, innocent, vulnerable, and trustworthy to those so-called intellects. Specially, in the case of the Moroccan artist/architect student who came from a well cultured family. His father worked with the Moroccan king, his older brother was the agriculture minister and he was studying architecture in Belgium but was not fully financially supported by them. Sometimes I had to pay for his examination fees for both himself and his room-mate who was also his live-in partner.

I discovered the truth when I took a trip to Brussels in Belgium to his place, I saw and learnt that he came shopping and robbed my little angels' food and pocket money to give to his live-in boyfriend. They were living like husband and wife. There was no place for me. Every time he wanted to visit me I paid for his return ticket and he was welcomed to my place in the UK he always came with emptied hands but left with bags of valuable goods. I only visited him for the day because there was no space for me in his one tiny rented bedroom which I helped out to pay his rent whenever the landlord threatened to evict him and his *pede,* gay-friend. The second time I paid him a surprise visit he was naked in bed with another French man. So I returned to my place very hurt.

It did not cross my mind that he was cheating on me by stealing my hard earned working money to provide for his live-in male partner. He took the food of my children to feed himself and his room-mate. One day he came to reveal his obsession with his live-in partner but had promised his mother to marry his cousin after he completed his architectural course and would work for his country. When I spoke to him early this year after I googled him I found he was practising his architectural work in Morocco. He spoke to me on skype and told me that he had married his cousin and he has 5 daughters. I wonder what he will do if one of his daughters meets someone who behaved like him when he was a student. I asked about his *'pede'* - gay, his live-in boyfriend who shared his life and studied with him in Belgium. He told me he is an unemployed alcoholic and is doing nothing. That shows you how selfish one can be. When he was lonely in Belgium his friend was his intimate company and he came to visit me in London to take my poor children money and food for both of them. Now he has his family and he doesn't care for his long time intimate male friend neither does he think about my children. I stopped to exist the moment he got graduated and went back to live in his country. Once I was there for his comfort and support to help him become a successful man. This kind of human being is really a human 'killing'. Money was not an issue for me at that time. Although I was not academically trained I had 3 skills such as shorthand typist office secretary, a medical secretary and a qualified nurse and I used to work using all these skills; at the same time I looked after my son and daughter to keep my house and car in London. At that same time, I was building a holiday house for my kids in Mauritius on my own piece of land I bought. Well, I did not mind him coming to beg for things which I had spare to share as my children were small, but I hated him taking electronic gadgets which were meant for my children. He bought and wore brand names while my children had to wear cheap clothes which I got from the local market.

I did not pay attention to his financial problems. I knew he told me he came from a very rich and famous family. What I couldn't understand why such an artistic person could not sell his works of art for extra money instead of coming to London nearly every weekend to enjoy visiting works of arts, to buy books in the biggest library. I had to pay for his brand named goods, books and electronic phone and camera which I did not have for myself. He stated that his works of art were exhibited freely in the museum of Brussels. He spoke fluent Arabic, a Muslim by name and knew the religion more than I did. Why a Muslim man should use and abuse another Muslim single mother with 2 children for finance and material gains only? I was amazed to discover that he was not ashamed to steal things from my property or even cash from my purse. His work of art was really weird. Today he has 5 daughters and I wonder how he will react if his daughters meet men like himself. Another thing I could not forget was one of his picture he drew of his mother hanging on his wall which reminded me of the people who practised black magic like the clairvoyants I saw when I was small in Mauritius. I was naïve and did not realise that he was playing a double life of living poor with me and the rich boy with his live-in partner He had very expensive taste, he planned and drew his designs of the clothes before going out shopping with me in London. Of course, I was the one who would foot the bills. When he went to my neighbour's and friend's party he was attracted by both the male and female guests.

When he came on Skype recently this year to speak with me live I saw in him an old bald selfish man whom I regret to have known and allowed to be used and abused by in my youth. I did not find in him the same most handsome artist/architecture student whom I met on my first holiday in Spain nearly 30 years ago. What a mistake I committed by sitting on his allocated seat and that moment I became one of his victims until he left Brussels to get married to his chosen bride by his mother. What a nightmare he was in my life then. I realize his greed and audacious character now I had to accept it as it was my fate. I became wiser and more cautious but again because of my nature I fell for another worse man to rub salt in my wound.

In the UK I was feeling hurt and frustrated and at that painful moment I met with someone who changed his name to Dawood simply because he claimed to have converted into Islam. We met at a college studying card reading. I did not know about my Muslim religion and my holy *Qur'an* which is the book of healing. I regret spending all my hard working money by making successful men who did not care about my children. I suffered together with my children tremendously. Even the Moroccan architect would not return a favour to help me to design a mosque or an Islamic centre for the poor and deprived children. This kind of project

49

is very beneficial for the religion of Islam. He forgot that if it was not for my help and my financial support he would not be where he is now. When I asked for a favour to use his skills of art and architecture to help the poor and needed he was enquiring if I could help him to come and perform hajj as it is very difficult for him to get entry to Saudi Arabia. I inclined to say yes, simply because this is an obligatory duty for every Muslim who is sane and can afford must execute this task as it is for Allah.

It is said that misfortune comes in three. So for the third time, my life became into a living hell on earth by Dawood, the pretended Muslim, the father of 2 of my daughters, who came to rent a room in my house which was paid by the local government and his weekly 'dole' money was used for his imported vitamins from USA. His food was provided by me. He, too, took advantage of my weakness and generosity and my Islamic faith to scrounge as much as he could. He too was a soft gentle and well-spoken person who would make it his job to correct anyone's mispronunciation of a word in English. While the Moroccan intellect was enlightening me with his work of art and his poetic French speaking and talked about work of great French philosophers, Dawood, an eccentric, clever scientific, paranormal and physic student who tried to impress me with his 'queen' English. This cunning pretended Muslim who became the father of my 2 daughters, didn't make it his business to steal from me and his parent but from his own daughters, He abandoned them and disappeared in Indonesia to hide away and avoid paying inheritance tax to the British Government and to pay monthly payment to the Child Support Agency. All the money he amassed from his parent's old age pension and saving from my house plus the large sum his late father left for his grandchildren's education he invested them all for long term interested In addition to this large sum his intimate friend the Jewish magician gave him a large sum for his daughters' education. He took that also and invested all in a long term fixed interest on which he is living happily in Indonesia in free accommodation he met on line on a marriage website. There he is pretending to be a Muslim but practising his psychic hobbies and meditating. He is enjoying free transport and free lodging just as he did with me for almost 35 years. I have been told that he is doing some occasional English editing for 50 pence per page not to get bored. It is almost 6 years he has been receiving interest on this large sum which he never worked for. He is holidaying and relaxing in the island of Indonesia keeping himself stress-free.

When he was living in my house on and off for almost 35 years, every morning he would inspect the skip for any electrical useful goods. He would shop for his books and clothes in a charity shop called Oxfam. He would ride his bike to college and universities to study for a few 'A' levels. Which he achieved all his subjects in grades A's and then some degrees in Sciences, Master in Math, Physics. He is smarter and more cunning than my previous abuser. This shameless and egoistic father came in my house during my absence to renew his Indonesian visa in the UK. He shared the place of his daughter's ex-boyfriend's place where he could meditate in return of doing some house chores, driving the old parents around and helping them doing their shopping and walking their dogs. He has no responsibility towards his daughters and no consideration and support for their education. He would make use of their computers to keep in contact with the people he stayed with in Indonesia. He cared for the people who is providing him with free room and food and transport to enjoy the island. How could he take some strangers shopping and temporarily looked after them while I witnessed the cruelty he did with his own old parents for 3 months he encouraged me to cook liquidized food for both his parent, when they were dying in hospital with cancer, so that he could cash their weekly pension which he invested in his various bank accounts, Now he is happily living on interests in Indonesia. He told his daughters there is no need to come to the UK for renewal of his visa because he can simply jump on the plane to the nearest little island and have his visa renewed. He doesn't have to pay expensive fare to come to the UK.

CHAPTER 5

SUCCESSES AND FAILURES

Love and married life was a failure for me. I suffered from lots of unpleasant psychological and physical abuses during my short married life, none of these effects broke me. On the contrary, it made me stronger and brought me closer to my God. I could only recall the sufferance, pains, and the agonies more than the good memories. The men used my religion and faith and my generosity to have children by me and leave me to take full responsibilities of the innocent children who came to this world out of lies, cheats and promises. I survived and overcame all the obstacles only by Allah's Blessing, Help, Guidance and Mercy.

One thing I am thankful for is that I did not end up in a mental home because I took control of my long one parent or single motherhood life just as my mother did with her 8 children without any academic skills and job or career and without any of the new technology, such as a telephone, television, car and any help from the government. I succeeded in achieving and owning all the things that my mother was deprived of, simply by working, studying hard and having various academic skills. I held 4 jobs at the same time working as a qualified nurse at night, as Medical secretary, executive secretary in a bank in the day time and in the evening worked as a typist with a private contractor in order to support both my children and my au pairs who looked after them while I was practising all my skills. I also had opportunity to travel abroad and work as a teacher after I read my B.A (hons), MA, PGCE, CELTA and for my MA in Islamic Studies which helped me to understand my religion that I was born into.

I travelled overseas and worked unlike my mother who never travelled prior to her death. The only time she travelled was when I invited her to have a better life in the UK. Sadly, she did not make it as she succumbed to her illness and died peacefully in her sleep in the hospital. Really, she was used as a guinea pig and left to die without any of us being at her side. She left her native country to die as a foreigner in the UK in the late 70's.

Her death brought the end of my marriage due to the previous conflicts I was encountering with my ex in- laws' interference and racism. I was never welcomed in that family and my ex-husband used to love his family more than himself and perhaps more than me as his wife. I felt he did not do his duty as a husband towards me when I married him. He kept me in his one room in the male campus whenever I visited him on my day off. I was like a visitor during the weekends and days off only.

I was not happy and I found he was cheated on me while I was far away in my female campus in another district. I learnt how to drive and bought a car so I could go to visit him on my days off. Sometimes, his days off were different from mine. I stayed secretly in his room until his return from duty. I could not take any more of this suppression, I found excitement in one of my patient, who was a surveyor and was planning to go to South Africa. He had blood cancer and was a white South African supporter of apartheid system. His intimacy was very discreet. I had seen the countryside area both at night and days by driving his sport car. We saw most of West Sussex at night by long drive. It was exciting and exhilarating to see the beauty spots such as the seaside around the south of England and Beachy Head which was an attracted spot to look at but rather gloomy because most of the suicidal cases drowned their sorrows by simply jumping into its water from the high cliff.

We went out to eat in different cafés and restaurants. I enjoyed his company more than the food at that time. If my husband had treated me like a wife I would not have sought happiness and excitement from other people. Besides, he did not care what I was doing while he was entertaining himself with his friends at work in the mental hospital.

It was easy for me to break up my marriage without regret or remorse. When there is no respect, understanding and love in a relationship it is better to end it up. I did get hurt when my ex-husband messed about with my best friend's sister. They all made me feel that I was too black and too ugly for my husband. That is why I appreciated the one who was a supporter of the apartheid system person who treated me with respect and showed me what freedom and happiness was. Until now I feel that I will never meet a pious husband who takes care of his family like my father did. Well, maybe I have to believe in what my professor of Islamic studies said to me that I have to wait for the hereafter God's willing! God will create my pair for me in heaven if I did not have one here on earth.

Last year, I went to perform *hajj* - pilgrimage for my late loving brother who was murdered by our neighbours for going out with a married woman.

On my return to the hajj I suffered from a blister on my big toe which became infected due to the neglect of the nurses in the Saudi hospitals. Two of my toes on my left foot required amputation to save my foot. The doctor claimed it was due to my uncontrolled diet as I am diabetic.

This diabetes is a hereditary disease but I believed it was some nurses who used an unsterilized pair of forceps to remove my black nail and then picked on the bone under my toes. As a consequence, I had to lose 2 of my toes. Being a qualified nurse, I knew it was the fault of some Philippines nurses' carelessness.

I was fortunate to have a Lebanese caring doctor who saved my leg with his surgeon friend. I am so grateful to them for looking after me for the sake of *Allah, Alhamdulillal* - praise be *Allah*. For this tender loving care which I was lucky to have at such a great moment. I am also very fortunate to work in a small place where everybody is like a family. Some of my colleagues offer to carry my bag for me and the drivers who live next door always carry my heavy bags for me to my room.

As compared to all these nice helpers at hand, my daughter who was in Medina came to pay me a visit during my convalescent period. Her visit did not help because she left me with another bag with her stuff to carry with me to my home with my bad foot. My best friend was there to help. She is from Canada. I am blessed to have such a good, kind and caring friend. As for my daughter I had to carry her load with me 400 miles away from Riyadh, the capital of Saudi Arabia. Also on my return to Dammam my youngest daughter came to visit me from London. She gave more stress. I had a pillow thrown at me while snoring in my sleep because I was disturbing her from speaking to her friends in London. On the day of her departure, she wet the floor of the bathroom which caused me to fall and knocked my head on the wall. My best friend reminded her that we had a friend who had a broken ankle and she fell on head coming out the shower and she died on the spot. She reminded my youngest daughter that I was lucky that I did not suffer the same consequence.

Allah is great as I did not lose my foot. One of my daughters' behaviour caused more pain than my recent amputation of my toes during her short stay by refusing to pray and remained on her iPhone 24/7 with her friends from London. She would go shopping to take pictures to send them. She would spend all night talking to them. She did not give any attention to me. She was constantly making noise with her broken spare phone which I did not think of fixing it for her. I felt bullied by her and she was a constant threat to me when I told her to be quiet.

My second daughter, K, who has her father's characteristics, quits her Computer science degree, and has been working and wasting all her earnings on heavy drugs. Like her father who stayed in my house, she is doing exactly the same on the promise that she will pay me back one day.

In the meantime, she is enjoying her life travelling the world, driving her brand new in Europe and indulging on expensive drugs, and drinks to beat up her depression. She is selfishly happy and wishing me dead so life could be better for her. Despite many visas sent to her to visit me in Saudi, she did not care to come because she cannot do what she is doing in London such as driving is prohibited in Saudi and girls are segregated from boys. Walking alone on the streets is forbidden. Despite all the problems she has promised to visit me soon.

Last year, she went to Peru in South America spending all her savings then missed her returned flights many times she threatened to throw herself on the cliff. I had to rescue her because her father in Indonesia could not afford to send her money as he has his large fund on fixed interest. I sent her the money and she came back staying for free in my house.

After she returned to UK, as I was going to Mauritius for my holiday, she asked me to pay for her ticket so that she could help me on my journey as I have some problem with my foot. I had help from the airline. She was able to come with me. Like her father she wanted entertainment while others have to pay.

She fell in love with her cousin and went to stay away at her aunt's place to enjoy herself. She only came to my place to collect her belongings and flew back to the UK without me. Well, as soon she was in the UK she had forgotten about her cousin. As far as she is concerned, if I am dead, life would be a better for her.

She doesn't speak with her siblings she expects them to look after her by cooking and looking after her and her cat. She is a carbon copy in her look and character of her father. I wish them both happiness because they both have the philosophy of being happy and thinking of good things only. She is over stressed while her father is stress free.

I have to pay for the house she is at the moment enjoying despite all the stress I am going through. I must admit that I am the happiest and most peaceful with my prayers and my holy Book on my own. Life for me is so beautiful that I do enjoy staying alone. Dawood, a white British man who despises his country and hates to work for his country, believes that his late parents worked and paid tax to the government, therefore, he should contribute to his society.

He had travelled the world with his father who paid for everything. Until his father was bound to a wheelchair, life became more pleasant for him as they have the same first name and middle name and surname he was using his father credit cards and lives life more comfortably. He was not trusted by his late father. That is why his father sold the house in France to me for a little sum on his dying bed in hospital. As the contract was not completed legally, until now Dawood has not transferred the house on my name yet, he is holding on to it although I have all the documents of the house with me. Despite that my daughter K, who echoes her father's trait was brought up and taught Islamic studies by me and my friends, I wonder why she would behave exactly like her father. I discovered she was lying and cheating by not going to the 'Qur'anic School but went with her Buddhist boyfriend walking the streets of London. She even went to stay at her father's place at his magician's lodging with her boyfriend. That is why when he came for a short visit 2 years ago to renew his visa to Indonesia he stayed at her ex boyfriend's place in exchange of doing some house chores and driving for them.

Like my father I suffered similar fate. I had to support my 2 generations of children whom I brought up and educated on my own. I built a house for them and left my home to go abroad to pay for the bills in order they can stay and study. Unfortunately, they behave the same way my siblings did with my hard working pious father. I tried to follow the steps of my father even at a late stage.

The final blow in my life was to trust people who claimed to have converted into Islam religion. I was scammed by someone from Nigeria 401 who came on line on the promise that he would help my charity company if I help him out financially. He also promised he would build a mosque and a school for the people in my country. Therefore I took a loan and lent it to him. He disappeared with this large sum and I was left to pay back to the bank until now. It made me stronger and never doubted my religion. I persevered to work hard and have faith in my God and until today I am continuing to work hard. I went to Saudi Arabia in order to keep the house for my children to stay until they complete their study and after they get a well-paid job I can transfer the house in their names but none of them is willing to work until now. They are all living free and enjoying life doing what is keeping them happy.

I held on to my prayer and supplication which is keeping me going. I supported my children and tried to make them understand my religion to make them strong as my father and myself. They went against me. They used me and abused me like my siblings used to behave with my mother. I tried to live peacefully away from them and whenever I am with them for a short while I feel I am being harassed and terrorised by them.

I feel happy and peaceful without any of them around. I have a fear in me that when I grow older and become invalid how they will treat me. So I pray to God to take me before I become invalid and without pain like He took my father. Sadly, all of my children have spent all their money on hard drugs to hurt me but they did not realise they had hurt themselves. I am so thrilled to be away from them. I hope to have the same fate as my father not to have any of them around me.

My faith has helped me to be in control of my situation I did not need help from any psychiatrist or any mental hospital. Funny enough, both Dawood and his daughter K would still insist that I was mentally ill. His accusation in the court to win the custody of my daughters did not materialize because my medical reports from my doctor proved him wrong. I won my case of full custody of his 2 daughters only by seeking help and supplicating to my Creator. The most powerful words from my holy Qur'an chapter 2 verse 255: *in the name of Allah, the most Gracious, the Most Merciful 'There is no deity except Him, the Ever-Living, the Sustainer of [all] existence. Neither drowsiness overtakes Him nor sleep. To Him belongs whatever is in the heavens and whatever is on the earth. Who is it that can intercede with Him except by His permission? He knows what is '[presently] before them and what will be after them, and they encompass of a thing of His knowledge except for what He wills. His Kursī (Throne) extends over the heavens and the earth, and their preservation tires Him not. And He is the Most High, the Most Great.* These were the most powerful words I read during the court decision.

This was enough for the young judge to conclude the case by questioning Dawood with his final decision. He concluded by reprimanding Dawood by the following questions. How can you look after your daughters without a job and a place for them to live? As you are a permanent student will you have time to spend with your daughters? Will you be able to take them on holiday?

The Judge said to him, 'the mother has been working hard to provide your young daughters with education and took them on holiday abroad and kept a shelter over their head both in the UK and in Mauritius'. I was granted full custody while he gained access to them on restricted order. When he had them on alternate weekends he stayed at his parents most of the time in the suburb of London and when he was not with them he stayed with his Jewish magician friend which I discovered just before he planned to go in hiding to Indonesia.

He hid his address in Indonesia not to pay Child Support Allowance to his two daughters. He is living in a state of denial thousands of miles away from his responsibility.

Islam says that a true Muslim should not kill any creature of *Allah* but save a life instead. *Allah* says in His *Qur'an* that if one saves a life is like saving the whole world and if one kills another of His beings is like killing the whole nation. Here we have Dawood who meditates all the time but have no time to think about his own daughters. As a believer one has to follow the commands of Allah as mentioned in the Holy Qur'an to get into paradise. For example, building a mosque, learning and teaching the holy '*Qur'an*' and writing a book of knowledge are some acts which can benefit others. Well, by writing this book I hope it will help others who went through the same hardship as a single mother.

We can only give the message of Islam to someone but *Allah* is the One who chooses whom, when, where and how to give His religion and guidance. We are here just to convey the message which His last Prophet (pbuh) left to his disciples and all Muslims by learning from all his sayings and actions he left for us to follow. The prophet (pbuh) was described about his character as a walking Qur'an by one of his wives. That is the reason I chose two of my passions to build a mosque in my country of origin and to write a book about how I jumped over so many hurdles in life to become stronger in my faith. Islam is not only word but action and a way of life to get nearer and closer to *Allah,* Insha'Allah - God's Willing.

CHAPTER 6

APPRECIATE LIFE AND BE THANKFUL TO MY CREATOR

I would like to end this book by mentioning a beautiful supplication I love to read in my last prayer before going to sleep. The transliteration in Arabic and its meaning in English goes like this.

In the Name of Allah, the Most Gracious, the most Merciful.

Allahumma inna nasta inuka wa nastadiki wa nastarghhfiruka wa natubu ilaika wa nu'minu bika wa nuthni 'alayka wa nu'minu bika wa natawakkalu 'alaika wa nuthni 'alaika khaira kullahu, wa nashkuruka wa la nakfuruka. Wa nakhla 'u wa natruku man yafjuruka. Allahumma iyyaka na'budu. Wa Laka nusalli wa nasjudu, wa ilaika nas'a wa nahfidu, narju rahmataka wa nakhsha 'adhabaka, inna'adhaba kaljidda bilkuffari mulhaqun. Ameen

The translation in English is 'O *Allah*! We ask for your help and guidance, we ask for Your forgiveness, we turn to You in repentance, we believe and trust in You, You are the source of everything good for us, hence we are thankful and grateful to You and leave those who commit sins and indulge in disbelief. O *Allah*! We worship only You, and for You alone we pray and prostrate to, we strive to please You, we expect Your mercy and fear Your punishment, and indeed Your severe punishment will befall on the blasphemers.' Amen

Also it is important to protect oneself from evil that possesses innocent human beings by reading 3 times those chosen verses which my father taught me when I was small. First when I felt scared at night, he told me to recite that 'there is no power but *Allah* and He is the greatest'. Followed by the 3 last chapters in the holy 'Qur'an' 112,113 and 114. These verses he advised me to memorise and repeat them when I had nightmares and got scared at night. These are the following verses in transliteration from Arabic. First,

I must always start by saying 'Bismisllahir Rahmanir Rahim, then followed by '*Walla Hawla WA La Quwata Illilah billah*' - there is no power but *Allah* and He is the greatest. Second followed by the 3 last chapters in the holy Qur'an 112,113 and 114.

'*Bismisllahir Rahmanir Rahim, Qul huuwallahu ahad, Allahu samad. Lam yalid wa lam yulad. Wa lam yakul lahu kufuwan ahad* - In the name of *Allah*, the most Merciful, the most Kind. Say, He is *Allah*, the One. *Allah* is Eternal and Absolute. None is born of Him nore is He born. And there is none like Him. The holy *Qur'an*, chapter 112. This is one of the shortest verses in the Book of Allah and it is worth one third of the book. It tells us about the attributes of Allah. So whenever someone asks me who Allah is. I recite this verse as Allah describes himself in His Holy Book, the Qur'an.

The next verse must be read trice when also to heal a possessed person from jinns (evils) *Bismillahir rahmanir Rahim. Qul a'adhu bi rabbil falaq. Min sharri ma khalaq. Wa min sharri ghasiqi idha waqab. Wa min sharrin naffathati fil 'uqad. Wa min sharri hasiden idha hasad*' - In the name of *Allah*, the Most Merciful, the Most Kind. Say, I seek refuge in the Lord of the Daybreak;, from the evil of what He has created; from the evil of darkness when it is intense; from the evil of those who seek to promote discord (malignant witchcraft); from the evil of the envier when he envies.' Chapter 113.

Ending up with the last chapter of the Holy Qur'an, which is *'Bismillahir rahanir Rahim. Qul a'uthu birabbin nas. Malikin nas. Ilahin nas. Min sharril wasuwasil khannas. Allazi yuwasawisu fi sudurinas. Minsal jinnati wannas.'* - In the name of Allah, the most Merciful and the Most Kind. Say, I seek refuge in the Lord of mankind, the God of mankind, from the mischief of the sneaking whisperer, who whispers in the hearts of mankind, from among jinn and mankind.' Chapter 114. The other one of my favourite which has been the greatest help in my most difficult times was the verse 255 in chapter 2. It is called the Ayat-ul-Kursi or the throne of Allah and it goes as follows:

'in the name of Allah, the most Gracious, the Most Merciful. ***There is no deity except Him, the Ever-Living, the Sustainer of [all] existence. Neither drowsiness overtakes Him nor sleep. To Him belongs whatever is in the heavens and whatever is on the earth. Who is it that can intercede with Him except by His permission? He knows what is '[presently] before them and what will be after them, and they encompass of a thing of His knowledge except for what He wills. His Kursī*** *(Throne) extends over the heavens and the earth, and their preservation tires Him not. And He is the Most High, the Most Great.'*

By simply reciting these words protect me and help me to gain the things I needed most in my life. The first time when I was in my crisis in the Island of Grenada I had no money. I was given help to ship my cargo freely to the UK. The second time was when I was defending my case in the magistrate court to keep my daughters versus Dawood who was interested to win the case to hand them to his obsessed Jewish fake magician for experiment on the power of metal bending and thirdly when I lost my small beautiful little tape recorder which had the first word of my baby daughter in it. I happened to lose it in a big park called Finsbury Park where it was impossible to find it. I went the next morning and I met with the park keeper who told me the sweeper found it and gave it to him. After describing the tape recorder to him, he gave it to me. In fact, yesterday I lost the butterfly from my left diamond earring. I spent most of the night looking for it but in vain. In the morning, I prayed and read the verse of 'the throne of Allah'. I pulled the sofa which was far away from where it dropped I found it. Some several years ago, I also found an engagement ring of my children's teacher in a swimming pool by reading this verse. It was amazing as to how I found those lost items which were impossible to find. In fact, I met with a young Saudi healer last year he too taught to remove bad jinns from the possessors by reading this verse of Ayat-ul-Kursi 10 times and 3 times all the 3 chapters 112, 113 and 114 and blow on the possessor. The jinn will leave his or her victim or accept the Islam religion and stop doing harm to any Muslim believer.

The following words were given as a gift by our prophet's (pbuh) to his favourite daughter Fatima (May Allah be pleased with her), instead of a slave to help her with hard chores at her house such as grinding the maize. She was advised to read the following words: 33 '*Subhan Allah*' meaning praise be to *Allah*; 33 '*Alhamdullilah*' glory to *Allah*, and 34'*Allah o Akbar*' - *Allah* is the Greatest which make a total of 100 altogether. By remembering these and repeating these praising words of Allah after each prayer I feel the heaviness of any of my chores become lighter and easier.

I practise Islam. The civil conversations in life and faith are related to each other. Faith relates honesty, integrity, modesty, responsibility and grateful living. Faith understands to be kind to a life of the taciturn sufferer.

I would like to end with the most beautiful names of Allah as shown below and I am told if a Muslim believer memorizes these names and recites them every day. The reciter will be guaranteed paradise. The Prophet (pbuh) said: "Allah the Most High has ninety-nine names. He who retains them in his memory will enter Paradise." He also said:

"No-one is afflicted by distressed or anxiety then invokes Allah with this supplication, but Allah will take away his distress and grant him or her happiness instead."

He is Allah, there is none worthy of worship except for Him. These are His 99 names:

1.	Ar-Rahman	The compassionate
2.	Ar-Rahim	The Merciful
3.	Al-Malik	The King
4.	Al-Quddus	The /Holy
5	As-Salam	The Giver of Peace
6.	Al-Mu'min	The Giver of Security
7.	Al-Muhaymin	The Protection
8.	Al-Aziz	The Mighty
9.	Al-Jabbar	The Compeller
10.	Al-Mutakabbir	The Majestic
11.	Al- Khaliq	The Creator
12.	Al- Bari	The Maker
13.	Al-Musawwir	The Fashioner
14.	Al-Ghaffar	The Great Forgiver
15.	Al-Qahhar	The Dominant
16.	Al-Wahhab	The Bestower
17.	Al-Razzaq	The Provider
18.	Al-Fattah	The Opener
19.	Al-'Alim	The All-Knowing
20.	Al- Qabid	The Restrainer/Withholder
21.	Al-Basit	The Plentiful Giver/Expander
22.	Al-Khafid	The Humiliator
23.	Ar-Rafi'	The Exalter
24.	Al-Mu'izz	The Honourer
25.	Al-Muzil	The Humiliator
26.	As-Sami'	The All-Hearing

27.	Al-Basir	The All-Seeing
28.	Al-Hakam	The Judge
29.	Al-'Adl	The Just
30.	Al-Latif	The Subtle
31.	Al-Khabir	The All-Aware
32.	Al-Halim	The Indulgent or Clement
33.	Al-Azim	The Most Great
34.	Al-Ghafur	The Forgiving
35.	Ash-Shakur	The Grateful
36.	Al-'Ali	The Most High/Sublime
37.	Al-Kabir	The Great
38.	Al-Hafiz	The Preserver
39.	A-Muqit	The Nourisher
40.	Al-Hasib	The Reckoner/Bringer of judgement
41.	AlJalil	The Exalted/The Majistic
42.	Al-Karim	The Bountiful
43.	Ar-Raqib	The Watcher
44.	Al-Mujib	The Responsive
45.	Al-Wasi'	The All-Embracing/The Omnipresent
46.	Al-Hakim	The All-Wise
47.	Al-Wadud	The Loving
48.	Al-Majid	The All-Gorious
49.	Al-Ba'ith	The Raiser/Resurrector
50.	Ash-Shahid	The Witness
51.	Al-Haqq	The Truth
52.	Al-Wakil	The Trustee/Advocate
53.	Al- Qawiy	The Strong
54.	Al-Matin	The Firm/The Streadfast
55.	Al-Wali	The Protecting Friend
56.	Al-Hamid	The All –Praiseworthy
57.	Al-Muhsi	The Accounter
58.	Al-Mubdi'	The Initiator/Originator
59.	Al-Mu'id	The Reproducer/Restorer

60.	Al-Muhyi	The Giver of Life
61.	Al-Mumit	The Giver of Death
62.	Al-Hayy	The Living
63.	Al-Qayyum	The Self-Subsisting/The Independent
64.	Al-Wajid	The Perceiver
65.	Al-Majid	The Glorious/The Magnificent
66.	Al-Wahid	The Unique
67.	Al-Ahad	The One/The Indivisible
68.	As-Samad	The Absolute/The Self-Sufficient
69.	Al-Qadir	The All-Powerful
70.	Al-Muqtadir	The Dominant
71.	Al-Muqaddim	The Promoter/Expediter
72.	Al-Mu'akhkhir	The Retarder/The Delayer
73.	Al-Awwal	The First
74.	Al Aakhir	The Last
75.	Az-Zahir	The Manifest
76.	Al-Batin	The Hidden/The Unmanifest
77.	Al-Wali	The Patron/Governor
78.	Al-Muta'ali	The Supremely Exalted
79.	Al-Barr	The Beneficent/The Good
80.	AlTawwab	The Relenting/The Ever-Returning
81.	Al-Muntaqim	The Avenger,
82.	Al-'Afu	The Pardonner
83.	Ar-Ra'uf	The Compassionate/The Kind
84.	Malik-ul-Mulk	The Owner of all Sovereignty
85.	Zul-Jalali-Wal-Ikram	The Lord of Majesty and Bounty
86.	Al-Muqsit	The Equitable
87.	Al-Jami'	The Gatherer
88.	Al-Ghani	The Rich/The Self-Sufficient
89.	Al-Muhgni	The Emancipator/The Enricher
90.	Al-Mani'	The Withholder
91.	Ad-Darr	The Distresser
92.	An-Nafi	The Benefactor

93.	An-Nur	The Light
94.	Al-Hadi	The Guide
95.	Al-Badi'	The Incomparable, The Unattainable
96.	Al-Baqi	The Everlasting/The Infinite
97.	Al-Warith	The Heir/The Inheritor
98.	Al-Rashid	The Guide to the Right Path
99.	As-Sabur	The Patient

The End

Alhamdullilah (Praise to Allah)

Printed in the United States
By Bookmasters